DEAR SOUL,

WE HOPE THAT COLORING IN OUR MINDFULNESS COLORING BOOK WILL BRING YOU MUCH JOY AND NURTURE YOUR SPIRIT.

WHETHER YOU'RE NAVIGATING THROUGH MOMENTS OF ANXIETY, SEEKING SOLACE IN TIMES OF SADNESS, OR JUST LOOKING FOR A MOMENT TO RELAX, IT SERVES AS A GENTLE SANCTUARY, GUIDING YOU TOWARD A SERENE STATE OF MIND AND HEART.

LET THE HARMONIOUS DESIGNS AND TRANQUIL PATTERNS INFUSE YOUR WORLD WITH A SPRINKLE OF JOY, BRINGING A SMILE TO YOUR FACE AMIDST LIFE'S CHALLENGES.

THANK YOU FOR CHOOSING OUR MINDFULNESS COLORING BOOK. MAY THE GENTLE HUES, SOOTHING AFFIRMATIONS, AND INSPIRING QUOTES WITHIN ITS PAGES ILLUMINATE YOUR PATH TO INNER PEACE AND CONTENTMENT.

WITH HEARTFELT WISHES
FOR TRANQUILITY AND INNER HARMONY,
DAISY KINGSMAN

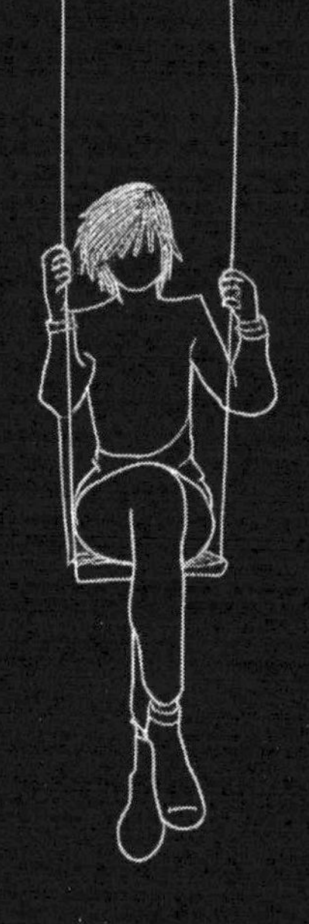

In the delicate dance of colors and patterns,
we uncover a tranquil pause where time softly drifts away
Each hue weaves a thread of serenity, guiding us gently
back to the calm within. Let this creative journey
be a quiet practice of mindfulness, where every stroke
whispers peace and presence.

COLOR SWATCH TEMPLATE

THIS BOOK
BELONGS TO: . . ______ ♡ ______ . .

One day
at
a
time

SELF CARE SHELF

I'M FREE FROM THE OPINIONS
AND JUDGEMENTS OF OTHERS

BE HOPEFUL WHEN THINGS ARE BAD
BE HUMBLE WHEN THINGS ARE GOOD

In the darkness,
even the tiniest star radiates its light

Focus on
what matters

Collect
moments
Not
things

I CAN GET THROUGH ANYTHING
I BELIEVE IN ME
I AM ENOUGH
I LOVE MYSELF
POSITIVE TEA
I AM CAPABLE
Tea is a hug in a cup
I AM STRONG
I AM
ESILIENT
I DESERVE GOOD THINGS
I AM GRATEFUL
I AM WORTH IT

Mostly, the world sees me

the way I see myself

Learn to pause and observe.

PLANT KINDNESS

HARVEST LOVE

IT IS OKAY,
NOT TO
BE OKAY.
SOMETIMES,
ALL YOU
CAN DO
IS
HANG
IN
THERE,
AND
THAT
IS
OKAY.

Inhale calm, exhale doubt

GETTING
LOST IS THE
GREAT WAY
TO FIND
YOURSELF

When you find yourself in a dark place,
you may feel you've been buried.

I am surrounded by love, support, and positive energy

YES
YOU CAN

Life is a journey not a race
CARE
SMILE
LIVE
GROW
LAUGH
LOVE
DREAM
HOPE

Advice from cacti
Get plenty of sunshine
Be patient through the dry spells
Conserve your resources
Wait for your time to bloom
Stay sharp but sweet

MAKE TODAY SO AWESOME
YESTERDAY GETS JEALOUS

Difficult
paths
often
lead to
beautiful
destinations

Put
your
worries
in
bubbles
And blow
them
away

OverThinking keeps you busy
buT iT Takes you nowhere

Spoonful of FRIENDSHIP
Splash of JOY
Feather of HOPE
Sprinkle of MINDFULNESS
Dollop of TOLERANCE
Dash of LOVE
Cupful of LUCK
Handful of GRATITUDE
HAPPINESS POTION
Pinch of INSPIRATION

Just
when
the
caterpillar
thought
her life
was over
she began
to fly

Beauty resides in the unseen, awaiting discovery

YOUR ATTITUDE IS WHAT
DETERMINES YOUR DAY

Broken crayons

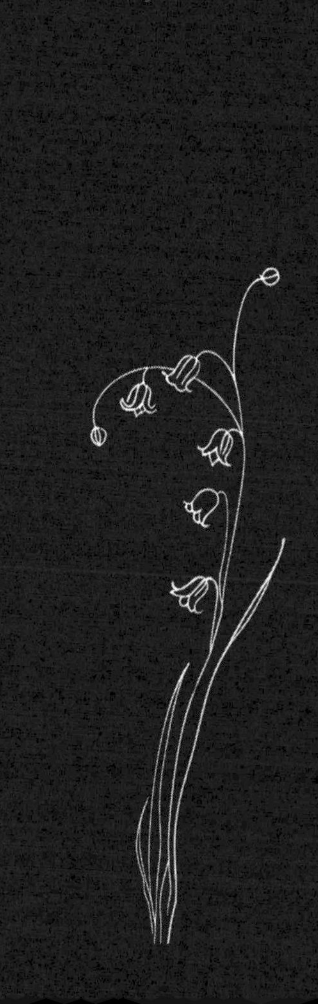

You can't
control
the wind
But you can
adjust your sails

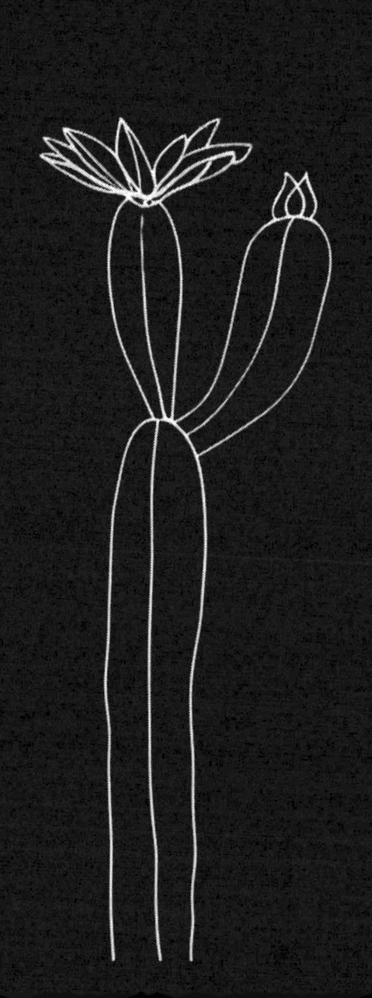

Anything
You think
Don't believe

Worrying does not take away tomorrow's trouble.
It takes away today's peace.

TRUST
THE
PROCESS
HONEY

GROW
POSITIVE THOUGHTS

Don't wait for
The perfect moments

Take The moments
and make Them perfect

LET GO OF THE
EXTRA BAGGAGE
YOU DON'T
NEED TO
CARRY
GRUDGES
GUILT
OTHERS' EXPECTATIONS
REGRETS
TOXIC RELATIONSHIPS
REJECTIONS

SEE THE
BEAUTY IN
EVERY TINY
BLOSSOM

I don't have to know everything
I'm doing what's best for me
I can make mistakes
I can say "No"
I can't please everyone
I am right
where I am meant to be

I'M FULLY
AT EASE

If it costs you your peace

it's too expensive

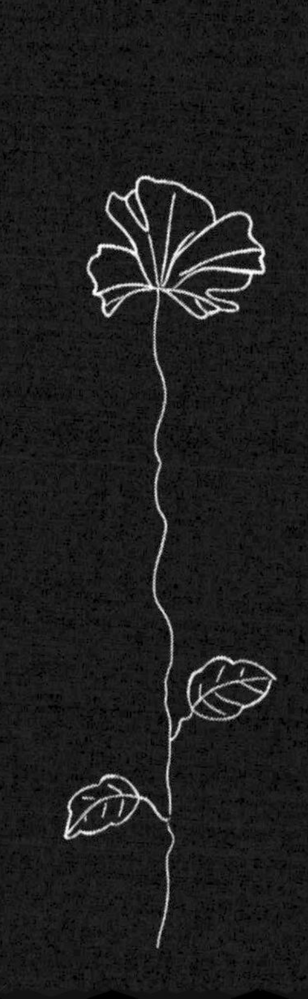

CHOOSE

HAPPY

The Intention Tree

Set your intentions, bring them to life with color, visualize them clearly, and let the universe take care of the rest.

Rainbow of Mindfulness Challenge

Each band and the clouds at the end of the rainbow represent a different mindfulness challenge, while the heart and other clouds can be dedicated to your challenges or simply coloring.

The tasks are designed to help you grow and connect with yourself. After completing each challenge, take a moment to reflect on your experience and color the corresponding band. Celebrate your progress and the positive changes you've made. Consider incorporating these mindfulness practices into your daily routine.

Mindful Eating: Eat one meal without any distractions—focus solely on the taste, texture, and aroma of your food.

Nature Connection: Spend an hour in nature. Focus on the smells, sounds, and sights around you.

Mindful Movement: Try yoga or tai chi, focusing on body-mind connection.

Digital Detox: Spend a day without social media or screens.

Gratitude Journaling: Write down three things you're grateful for each day for a week.

Self-Care Moment: Spend 15 minutes each day for a week doing something just for yourself

THE SKY OF WISHING STARS

Imagine your wishes filling the night sky. Write them in the stars, color them brightly, and let them inspire you every time you look up.

Joyful Moments
Let this page remind you of the happiness in your life. Write and color memories or moments that bring you joy. Notice how quickly you can complete this path and how wonderful your life truly is.

The Random Acts of Kindness Jar

Color in the symbols within the jar to represent
each of your kind deeds.
See how quickly you can fill the entire jar with color!

The Garden of Self-Love

Reflect on your best strengths and talents.
Write them in each heart, then color the flowers and petals.
As you do, let these thoughts comfort and uplift you.

5, 4, 3, 2, 1 ... A Simple Exercise To Calm Your Mind

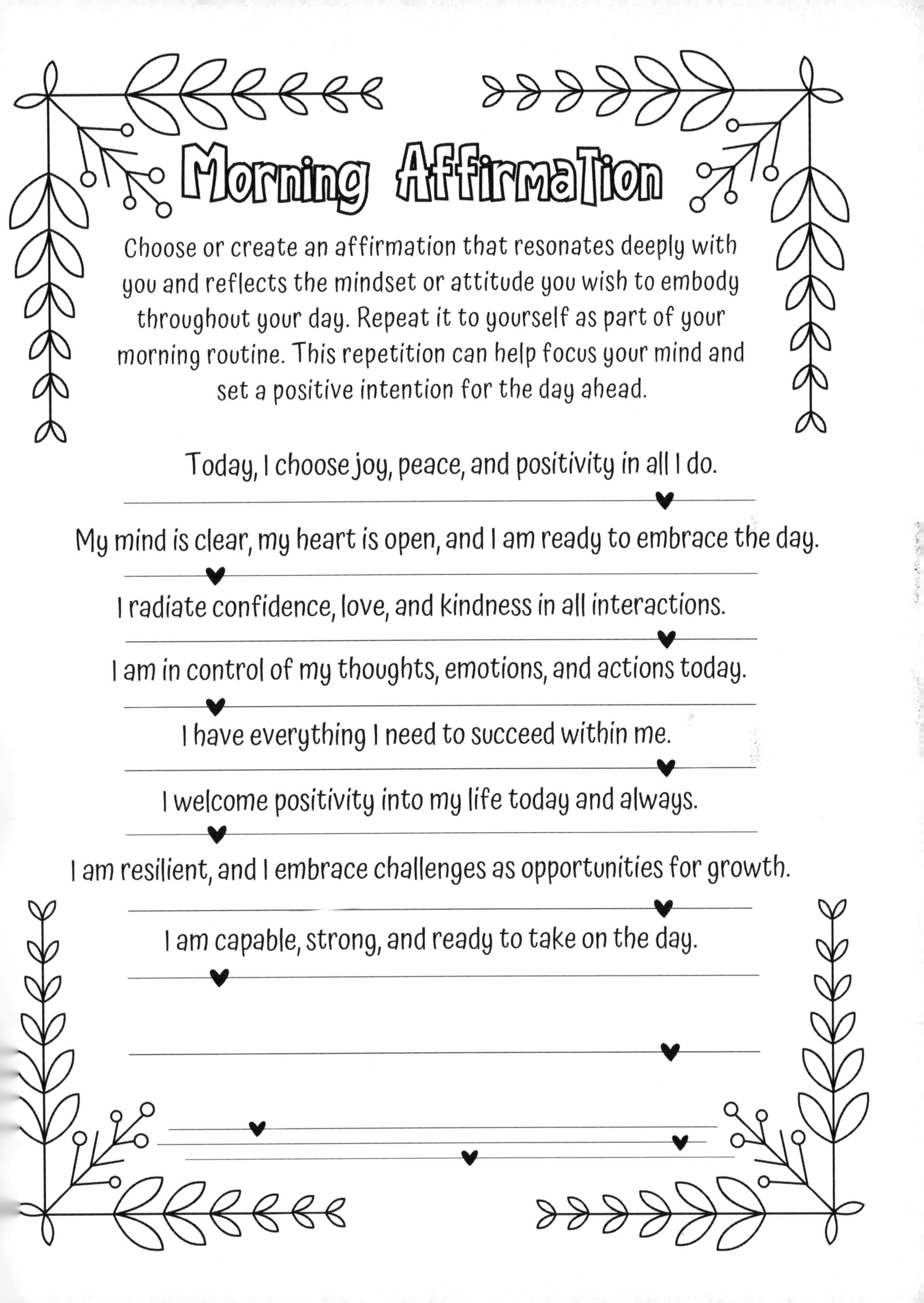

Morning Affirmation

Choose or create an affirmation that resonates deeply with you and reflects the mindset or attitude you wish to embody throughout your day. Repeat it to yourself as part of your morning routine. This repetition can help focus your mind and set a positive intention for the day ahead.

Today, I choose joy, peace, and positivity in all I do.

My mind is clear, my heart is open, and I am ready to embrace the day.

I radiate confidence, love, and kindness in all interactions.

I am in control of my thoughts, emotions, and actions today.

I have everything I need to succeed within me.

I welcome positivity into my life today and always.

I am resilient, and I embrace challenges as opportunities for growth.

I am capable, strong, and ready to take on the day.

5-Minute Meditation

Find a Comfortable Spot:

Sit or lie down in a relaxed position.
Close your eyes if you feel comfortable doing so.

Focus on Your Breath:

Take deep, slow breaths in through your nose and out through your mouth. Count to four as you inhale and four as you exhale.

Set an Intention:

Choose a positive affirmation or intention for this meditation.
Repeat it silently in your mind.

Visualize Calmness:

Imagine a serene place or a gentle, calming light surrounding you.
Let this image fill your mind and bring you peace.

Reflect:

Spend a few moments reflecting on how you feel. Acknowledge any thoughts that come up and gently bring your focus back to your breath and visualization.

In just five minutes,
you can find calm and clarity.
Breathe deeply,
center yourself,
and embrace tranquility.

Reflections & Notes

Reflections & Notes

Reflections & Notes

WOULD YOU LIKE SOME FREE GOODIES ?

PLEASE EMAIL ME AT:

DaisyKingsmanAuthor@gmail.com

Daisy Kingsman